HAL•LEONARD
INSTRUMENTAL
PLAY-ALONG

AUDIO
ACCESS
INCLUDED

TRUMPET

COLDPLAY

T0078817

Audio arrangements by Peter Deneff

Cover photo: Peter Neill – ShootTheSound.com

PLAYBACK+
Speed • Pitch • Balance • Loop

To access audio visit:
www.halleonard.com/mylibrary

"Enter Code"
2507-2948-5402-8477

ISBN 978-1-4768-1835-1

HAL•LEONARD®

Visit Hal Leonard Online at
www.halleonard.com

Contact Us:
Hal Leonard
7777 West Bluemound Road
Milwaukee, WI 53213
Email: info@halleonard.com

In Europe contact:
Hal Leonard Europe Limited
42 Wigmore Street
Marylebone, London, W1U 2RN
Email: info@halleonardeurope.com

In Australia contact:
Hal Leonard Australia Pty. Ltd.
4 Lentara Court
Cheltenham, Victoria, 3192 Australia
Email: info@halleonard.com.au

CONTENTS

CLOCKS

TRUMPET

Words and Music by GUY BERRYMAN,
JON BUCKLAND, WILL CHAMPION
and CHRIS MARTIN

IN MY PLACE

TRUMPET

Words and Music by GUY BERRYMAN,
JON BUCKLAND, WILL CHAMPION
and CHRIS MARTIN

EVERY TEARDROP IS A WATERFALL

TRUMPET

Words and Music by GUY BERRYMAN,
JON BUCKLAND, WILL CHAMPION, CHRIS MARTIN,
PETER ALLEN, ADRIENNE ANDERSON and BRIAN ENO

FIX YOU

TRUMPET

Words and Music by GUY BERRYMAN,
JON BUCKLAND, WILL CHAMPION
and CHRIS MARTIN

9

LOST!

TRUMPET

Words and Music by GUY BERRYMAN,
JON BUCKLAND, WILL CHAMPION
and CHRIS MARTIN

11

PARADISE

TRUMPET

Words and Music by GUY BERRYMAN,
JON BUCKLAND, WILL CHAMPION,
CHRIS MARTIN and BRIAN ENO

THE SCIENTIST

TRUMPET

Words and Music by GUY BERRYMAN,
JON BUCKLAND, WILL CHAMPION
and CHRIS MARTIN

SPEED OF SOUND

TRUMPET

Words and Music by GUY BERRYMAN,
JON BUCKLAND, WILL CHAMPION
and CHRIS MARTIN

TROUBLE

TRUMPET

Words and Music by GUY BERRYMAN,
JON BUCKLAND, WILL CHAMPION
and CHRIS MARTIN

VIOLET HILL

TRUMPET

Words and Music by GUY BERRYMAN,
JON BUCKLAND, WILL CHAMPION
and CHRIS MARTIN

YELLOW

TRUMPET

Words and Music by GUY BERRYMAN,
JON BUCKLAND, WILL CHAMPION
and CHRIS MARTIN

VIVA LA VIDA

TRUMPET

Words and Music by GUY BERRYMAN,
JON BUCKLAND, WILL CHAMPION
and CHRIS MARTIN

23

The Beatles

All You Need Is Love • Blackbird • Day Tripper • Eleanor Rigby • Get Back • Here, There and Everywhere • Hey Jude • I Will • Let It Be • Lucy in the Sky with Diamonds • Ob-La-Di, Ob-La-Da • Penny Lane • Something • Ticket to Ride • Yesterday.

00225330	Flute	$14.99
00225331	Clarinet	$14.99
00225332	Alto Sax	$14.99
00225333	Tenor Sax	$14.99
00225334	Trumpet	$14.99
00225335	Horn	$14.99
00225336	Trombone	$14.99
00225337	Violin	$14.99
00225338	Viola	$14.99
00225339	Cello	$14.99

Chart Hits

All About That Bass • All of Me • Happy • Radioactive • Roar • Say Something • Shake It Off • A Sky Full of Stars • Someone like You • Stay with Me • Thinking Out Loud • Uptown Funk.

00146207	Flute	$12.99
00146208	Clarinet	$12.99
00146209	Alto Sax	$12.99
00146210	Tenor Sax	$12.99
00146211	Trumpet	$12.99
00146212	Horn	$12.99
00146213	Trombone	$12.99
00146214	Violin	$12.99
00146215	Viola	$12.99
00146216	Cello	$12.99

Disney Greats

Arabian Nights • Hawaiian Roller Coaster Ride • It's a Small World • Look Through My Eyes • Yo Ho (A Pirate's Life for Me) • and more.

00841934	Flute	$12.99
00841935	Clarinet	$12.99
00841936	Alto Sax	$12.99
00841937	Tenor Sax	$12.95
00841938	Trumpet	$12.99
00841939	Horn	$12.99
00841940	Trombone	$12.99
00841941	Violin	$12.99
00841942	Viola	$12.99
00841943	Cello	$12.99
00842078	Oboe	$12.99

The Greatest Showman

Come Alive • From Now On • The Greatest Show • A Million Dreams • Never Enough • The Other Side • Rewrite the Stars • This Is Me • Tightrope.

00277389	Flute	$14.99
00277390	Clarinet	$14.99
00277391	Alto Sax	$14.99
00277392	Tenor Sax	$14.99
00277393	Trumpet	$14.99
00277394	Horn	$14.99
00277395	Trombone	$14.99
00277396	Violin	$14.99
00277397	Viola	$14.99
00277398	Cello	$14.99

Movie and TV Music

The Avengers • Doctor Who XI • Downton Abbey • Game of Thrones • Guardians of the Galaxy • Hawaii Five-O • Married Life • Rey's Theme (from Star Wars: The Force Awakens) • The X-Files • and more.

00261807	Flute	$12.99
00261808	Clarinet	$12.99
00261809	Alto Sax	$12.99
00261810	Tenor Sax	$12.99
00261811	Trumpet	$12.99
00261812	Horn	$12.99
00261813	Trombone	$12.99
00261814	Violin	$12.99
00261815	Viola	$12.99
00261816	Cello	$12.99

Popular Hits

Breakeven • Fireflies • Halo • Hey, Soul Sister • I Gotta Feeling • I'm Yours • Need You Now • Poker Face • Viva La Vida • You Belong with Me • and more.

00842511	Flute	$12.99
00842512	Clarinet	$12.99
00842513	Alto Sax	$12.99
00842514	Tenor Sax	$12.99
00842515	Trumpet	$12.99
00842516	Horn	$12.99
00842517	Trombone	$12.99
00842518	Violin	$12.99
00842519	Viola	$12.99
00842520	Cello	$12.99

Songs from Frozen, Tangled and Enchanted

Do You Want to Build a Snowman? • For the First Time in Forever • Happy Working Song • I See the Light • In Summer • Let It Go • Mother Knows Best • That's How You Know • True Love's First Kiss • When Will My Life Begin • and more.

00126921	Flute	$14.99
00126922	Clarinet	$14.99
00126923	Alto Sax	$14.99
00126924	Tenor Sax	$14.99
00126925	Trumpet	$14.99
00126926	Horn	$14.99
00126927	Trombone	$14.99
00126928	Violin	$14.99
00126929	Viola	$14.99
00126930	Cello	$14.99

Top Hits

Adventure of a Lifetime • Budapest • Die a Happy Man • Ex's & Oh's • Fight Song • Hello • Let It Go • Love Yourself • One Call Away • Pillowtalk • Stitches • Writing's on the Wall.

00171073	Flute	$12.99
00171074	Clarinet	$12.99
00171075	Alto Sax	$12.99
00171106	Tenor Sax	$12.99
00171107	Trumpet	$12.99
00171108	Horn	$12.99
00171109	Trombone	$12.99
00171110	Violin	$12.99
00171111	Viola	$12.99
00171112	Cello	$12.99

Wicked

As Long As You're Mine • Dancing Through Life • Defying Gravity • For Good • I'm Not That Girl • Popular • The Wizard and I • and more.

00842236	Flute	$12.99
00842237	Clarinet	$12.99
00842238	Alto Saxophone	$12.99
00842239	Tenor Saxophone	$11.95
00842240	Trumpet	$12.99
00842241	Horn	$12.99
00842242	Trombone	$12.99
00842243	Violin	$12.99
00842244	Viola	$12.99
00842245	Cello	$12.99

HAL•LEONARD®